A WOMAN IN THE

Photo: Alex Barlow

Evelyn Francis Capel

A Woman
in the
Priesthood

Evelyn Francis Capel

TEMPLE LODGE
London

First edition 1992

© Evelyn Francis Capel

All rights reserved. No part of this publication may be reproduced in any manner whatsoever without the prior permission of Temple Lodge Publishing, 51 Queen Caroline Street, London W6 9QL

The moral right of the author has been asserted

A catalogue record for this book is available from the British Library

ISBN 0 904693 42 2

Cover by S. Gulbekian. Inset: 'The Disputation of St Barbara', by permission of the British Library

Typeset by DP Photosetting, Aylesbury, Bucks
Printed and bound in Great Britain by Cromwell Press Limited, Broughton Gifford, Wiltshire

Acknowledgements

I wish to express my indebtedness to Stella Parton, who typed the manuscript. She also provided the Notes and References, with the aid of Peter Heathfield and other helpers at the Rudolf Steiner House library. I would also like to thank Eileen and Dan Lloyd for their valuable editorial help.

Summary of Contents

Foreword by the Rev. Dr. Martin Israel   xi

Prologue   The function and special characteristics of the priest, no longer solely a male prerogative. Consultation at the altar, with the divine will.   1

Chapter

1   Preparation for the priesthood in the writer's life, her ordination and early experiences.   5

2   Influence of women in pre-Christian religions. The divinity of Mary, worship of the Madonna. Mary, the mother and her guardianship. Divine will and human will (Egyptian and Greek examples). The influence of the saints.   10

3   Celtic Christianity, Celtic mythology. Great ladies of influence in the early Christian Church. Abélard and Héloïse and the development of human thought. Opposition between masculine and feminine. Man as fighter, woman as inspirer and comforter.   17

4	Changing human consciousness. Contrast between Queen Elizabeth I and Mary Queen of Scots. Feminine qualities much less distinguishable from male ones in modern times. The Ego, heroism—Sir Philip Sydney. Stevie Smith—poetry an expression of what was undertaken by her beyond the obligations of her ordinary life.	23
5	Mary Magdalene: washing the feet and annointing the head of Christ Jesus. His infinite forgiveness. Martha and Mary and the transformation of their forces of heart and will. Lazarus, representing the Ego, and the imparting of the forces of heart and will by the two sisters. The modern person containing these forces within the Self. The gift of the Holy Spirit and the awakening of the Apostles to the reality of what they had experienced. Distinctions between man and woman changing, opening to women the same faculties that were in past times associated solely with men.	29
6	The three tasks of the priest in the Christian Community. Raising the consciousness to celebrate the sacraments. Overcoming the limitations. Stevie Smith: her demonstration of working out her problems at the base of the 'Jacob's ladder' and making her decisions at the top. Her vision of Christ. Reconciliation of the Martha/Mary problem.	34

7   Second task of the priest: developing a further   39
    understanding of Christianity. St Brendan's
    voyage to find Paradise. The Book of
    Revelations and the future. Particular task of a
    new movement in Christianity to take up and
    continue the new ideas. Women's minds, as
    well as men's, are fitted for work in these
    fields. Christianity has no different rules for
    men, women, children or grown-ups. Christ's
    compassion for human souls. Reincarnation
    and Christianity. Making a new start in
    religious life.

8   Pastoral care, compared with confession to the   45
    priest. Methods of working discussed. Working
    with the principle of forgiveness. Comparison
    of the man's and the woman's approach and
    some difficulties each encounter. The priest's
    need for endurance, devotion and unselfishness.

Notes   50

Foreword

The insights of Rudolf Steiner, the son of a humble Austrian station-master, were to enrich many fields of human endeavour; to most of us his remarkable educational system is the best known, for Steiner had an innate feeling for psychologically disturbed children, and could produce positive results where conventional schooling failed. The secret was his belief in the ongoing process of the soul, limited as it might be in the present circumstances.

In the course of his life a philosophical system called Anthroposophy developed on the basis of his teaching, which in turn was the foundation of a church called the Christian Community. This was to be an international movement for religious renewal.

Evelyn Capel is a priest of the Christian Community, and her book considers the part women have played in the service of spirituality. The basis of ministry in the Christian Community is well described as is also the profound philosophy underlying the action of its sacraments. This book will be of use to those enquiring about the worship of the Christian Community. It also provides insights into women's ministry in the wider Church.

Martin Israel
London 1992

Prologue

What is the function of the priest? The answer to such a question takes us right back to the creation of the world, out of which as the highest achievement the creation of man has come. The first duty of man was to know and name the animals, the fish and the birds around him. The next experience of man was to discover his own double nature. Woman was created to share existence with him and to recognize her part in his life. Then came the serpent. Both Adam and Eve encountered temptation. Eve took the forbidden fruit first and gave it to Adam. The Fall into sin and evil was made known to the Creator, as they walked in the garden. They were expelled to live beyond the Garden of Paradise and to meet, in their experience on Earth, pain and suffering and the stress of hard work, but more came about through the generations of their children.

These became the bearers of human life and Cain could exert his will in destruction. Cain slew Abel and brought into the world the power of death. While Abel was the one who cared for the Earth and its life, Cain brought about inventions and the discoveries of human intelligence. The origin of this distinction was the need and duty of living creatures to offer in their lives to God that which came out of His gift to them. Through the discovery of death, an offering could be made of a living being, as Abel the shepherd had found. Cain imposed his will upon the Earth and, from his ploughing, the harvest of plants grew. In the second act of offering, man discovered how he could give to God. In creating the human world on Earth, man perceived how he could change the God-given world. Out of the offering of Abel, the life of the priest was born; out of the will of Cain, the man-created world arose. Priesthood was the invention of Abel; city building, the arts and the skills of war belonged to Cain.

It was not right that Cain's mastery over the whole world should go unchecked. Seth was therefore born to take the place of Abel. For the priest who would offer to carry the will of God into the affairs of the Earth, and to respond to it with offering, was as necessary as the vigorous power of action to change the world, demonstrated by Cain. The exertion of the human will in the history of mankind called for the reverence and respect of the human soul for the greater wisdom of God. The priest was as essential as the builder of cities. Reverence for the will of God was vital to creating man's world of Earth. In its modern variation it is found in the question: can there be morality among people without religion? In some great heroes of history the priest and the king were combined in one person, of which Melchizedek was the greatest example. But in earthly history there have been priests and kings side by side, the one devoted to reverence for the will of God and devotion to heavenly influences, the other making use of human will to change the surrounding world.

For as long as mankind has been divided into male and female, new life has come into the world through the mother. The power over death and destruction has been vested in the male, or the father. One of the oldest customs of pre-Christian times was connected with the birth of a child. Before the mother was allowed to feed him, or to take him into the life of the family, he had to be laid at the feet of the father who would then decide whether he was to be accepted into the family or left to die, that is, to be sent back to where he came from. The woman carried life and the man death. In the course of time human nature became changed. That which belongs to the true nature of the human soul began to descend into the sheaths produced for human life on Earth. The personal character has formed the life of soul in both men and women. In due course the spiritual being of man began to enter the individual person and to become stronger than the influence exerted on a man or a woman from the earthly side. Out of this transformation, modern experiences have arisen as symptoms. A wish is evident today to have a girl look like a boy and a boy look like a girl. Trousers are for everyone and a new term has been invented, 'unisex'. It is perhaps difficult to realize how these changes of custom have arisen, but within the soul's experience of life on Earth the conviction has arisen that the distinction between male and female characteristics should come to an end. Adam and Eve should unite in every person. Individuals are capable of every kind of wisdom and often enough of every kind of action. The special characteristic of the priest, that he turns to the wisdom of God as much as to his own, is no longer felt to be solely a male prerogative. It depends on who is capable of saying: do I need the heavenly wisdom of God as much as that of Earth, or is the earthly prowess of my mind more important? It is no longer a matter of the male or the female constitution, but of how far feeling and willing are capable of recognizing a heavenly or an earthly mission.

In the longer vision of human evolution, it is important that the heavenly capacities of the human soul should be given their due. Mankind can certainly be proud of human inventions and the changes they have brought into our lives on Earth. It was once felt that the changes brought about in the habits of life by artificial lighting, in street and home, enriched and extended the powers of the day. It is hard to imagine now the surrounding world without them. But has respect for the rhythm of life, in waking and sleeping, decreased? Is the wisdom given to the human soul in sleep more present in our decisions and actions than it would have been otherwise?

The question now is not whether a person can best experience devotion to the divine world while he or she is on Earth; it is more a matter of how far it is felt that the influence of the divine world is decreasing in the earthly. Is the egotism of today disturbing the balance of our human will between birth and death? Is it not necessary to say, 'the guidance of the divine will is needed in our life on Earth'? To be sensitive to it is essential to the priest, and the priest is essential to the proper development of human affairs. It is no longer the question: can a man or a woman achieve this better in modern life? The true question is: where are those who are willing to check their own egotism with a search for the divine will?

Actions performed at the altar are intended to be a consultation with divine will, which can bring higher wisdom into our earthly affairs. Those who feel that we are so clever nowadays, that we can do it all for ourselves, have ignored the question of life in the sacraments. How are we going to continue to consult the wisdom of God when we are so much involved with our earthbound intelligence? Each individual must decide out of the higher powers of his conscience. The thoughts of his true self will bring a better answer than the characteristic differences between male and female, between Adam and Eve.

1

When my university studies came to an end and I left Oxford, I embarked on life in London on my own, within the then very impressive and successful firm of Lyons. I learnt much through the experience of working with people of small education and a social background of a kind I had never encountered before. I learnt more socially than in the sphere of catering, which was in fact the purpose of the training that had been offered to me. Then came a shock of large proportions. The head of the firm, who was later to become famous for organizing the catering for the whole British Army in the Second World War, Isadore Gluckstein, offered me one of the best jobs that the firm could provide. It became obvious that it carried with it a very high standard of dedication to the purposes of the firm, which would call upon one's power of thought and feeling beyond the actual work one would do in the hours given to it. It offered a high level of worldly success, since at that time the firm's annual profits rose by the million. At the same time, it could be said that Lyons tea shops served the social needs of weary Londoners (their subsequent closure was felt as a loss by many). Yet, unusual methods of treating staff were also part of the firm's policy. As director for the tea shops section, Isadore himself would appear at any time, late or early, among the staff, taking a personal interest in what was going on. Meetings would be held at intervals for the whole staff of a shop, conducted and addressed by him. To a young onlooker, it seemed as if a representative of Jehovah was presiding over Judgment Day. It made a great impression on the staff.

When I thought about the amazing offer that had been made, I began to realize that the work involved would demand a dedication on my part which would invade my spiritual life. While being quite willing to devote the forces of spirit, soul and body in myself to a great purpose, I could by no means undertake to give such service for the general purposes of the firm of Lyons, or to those plans outlined to me in many individual conversations I had with the great man himself.

By that time I had become acquainted with the ideas and work of Rudolf Steiner.[1] His splendidly wide and high concept of the human being and of the value of human evolution had given me an idea of understanding and development such as I had never found before. I had met a number of personalities developing practical activities arising from this source and realized that it was possible to work with them. One was the most impressive teacher of children I had ever known. It was then that I came into contact with the Christian Community, a movement for religious renewal. Rudolf Steiner had assisted at its foundation in 1922 and initiated its practices. The movement was in the first stages of its development in Britain and in the use of the English language for its services. My upbringing had been in the Christian faith. I had been born in Stow-on-the-Wold, a small country town on a hilltop in the Cotswolds, where, small as it was, almost every expression of Christianity in a religious form could be found. My earliest experiences showed me what the grown-up people called 'the non-conformist conscience'. From the age of 2, I had known what it was like to sit in a pew during long, incomprehensible sermons, without envying the boy in the next row who was comforted by bananas. Such self-indulgence was not known in our pew.

In those days, many country dwellers had, like my grandmother, no other outlet of social enjoyment except religion. We had many conversations about which I early discovered the nature of doubt. Much Bible reading was carried on at home, but one day I learnt to read for myself and the first story I encountered was about the drunkenness of Noah. All the heroes of the Old Testament were brought to our acquaintance, instead of those of the traditional fairy-stories. I knew well that nothing would have disturbed my grandmother more than this event in the history of Noah, which had been withheld from me until I could read for myself. There was much to be learnt by reading the Bible oneself and also by my grandmother's prayers. But I was soon brought to realize how full of problems was the Christian religion. It included a row with one of my schoolteachers about whether the Pope's title deserved to be written by me with a capital P.

None of these experiences had made me enthusiastic about

Christianity, until I heard of Steiner's wonderful vision of Christ. He spoke of the Son of God descending to be the Son of Man and opening the door of human thinking, allowing our minds to grasp this fact in all its reality. The realization that we are citizens of the heavens along with that of the Earth and that we come and go, through birth and death, between Earth and Heaven, followed naturally. My mental horizon changed. I realized that the whole of human history is in reality Christianity. Christ created a pattern for the future evolution of humanity and it is our business to find and practise this within ourselves. We are in need of change and are longing for greater ideals. With this in mind, I could have taught children, but the most urgent need seemed to me to be to work with adults. At that time, the principles of training on the lines proposed by Rudolf Steiner had begun to operate, both in the field of general education, beginning with the founding of the Free Waldorf School in Stuttgart in the early 1920s, and in the Christian religion, out of which arose the founding of the Christian Community by ordained Lutheran clergy and other Protestant churchmen. I had another choice to make.

I attended the Seminar of the Christian Community in Stuttgart. At that time, no attempt was made to recognize the English language of myself or my companion, Stanley Drake, who subsequently became a priest. Help in this respect was given to us by Dr Friedrich Rittelmeyer, a leading clergyman of the Lutheran Church, who had resigned from that religious order to join the circle of those intent on founding the new movement for religious renewal. In time, I began to recognize my old acquaintances, the heroes of the Bible, in their German pronunciation.

The Christian Community is a movement for a new beginning in Christianity. It has sacraments, a theology and methods of pastoral care suitable for the developing consciousness of our time—but the eternal verities are maintained. It is an active undertaking in English-speaking countries and in middle Europe, and it is extending further. Everyone may attend services, but no prayer book is available. The experience of the spoken word is held to be important. When I undertook to work in this movement, the principle of the priesthood of women was already established, having been included at its foundation. So I became a pioneer in a new movement for the future form of Christianity.

Following my ordination I returned to England, just as the Second World War was beginning. I found the Christian Community in Britain to be small and impoverished in those days. Perhaps I had never quite realized the contrast between what I was offered by Isadore Gluckstein and that which came from Alfred Heidenreich, who was then the leader and pioneer of this new form of Christianity in Britain. America had not yet come into the picture. I had set out upon a path of adventure and come into a new movement for Christianity which had only begun a relatively short time before. I had met most of the founding priests, though not all. They told me that when, on the advice of Rudolf Steiner, Dr Rittelmeyer[2] had founded the Christian Community in Europe, three ladies had been present. The question came up of ritual and sacrament, and the concept of a new priesthood was a necessary consequence. The three women present did not expect to be called upon, but Rudolf Steiner himself said that in the event of Christianity being renewed the priesthood of women would be included. He gave as the grounds for this the new stage of human development. Without further argument this concept was accepted by everyone present, and no conflict of principle has arisen since.

The early history of the first three women priests was not a happy one. I heard of this later, when two of the first three ladies departed from their office. Convinced as they were at the beginning, they nevertheless strayed later on, perhaps because, in those days, they did not know how to handle their unique position in social life. For some time afterwards there was a natural reluctance in calling upon women to become priests. This was gradually overcome and the contribution made by more recent generations of women in the priesthood is praiseworthy. There is no evidence that the nature of women makes them unfit to be priests, or that they cannot make as worthy a contribution as their male colleagues. In any debate on the subject, matters of history play a bigger part than the evidence of the present. No debates of this kind have taken place in the Christian Community, but they often occur within the older churches. Those who oppose the priesthood of women do so because they are burdened with customs from earlier times. For myself, I have never been involved in such arguments, though I have experienced strange reactions from people at times. At a discussion on Christian theology, a canon of Westminster was present who must have disapproved when I was introduced to him as a lady priest, for he sat opposite to me in the circle and continued to pretend I was not there all afternoon. After a time I began to wonder if I was present myself! Some years later, I handed my passport to a customs official at Heathrow. He looked at it and said: 'You are in the fashion, aren't you?' In the course of time the concept of the priesthood of women has become natural and less remarkable. I shall now consider how the priesthood is becoming more and more suitable for women.

2

Women have not been priests in the Christian Church by appointment until this century. But they have, nevertheless, been a great influence in its development. In one sense, customs have continued which were in existence before the coming of Christ. Among the first Roman kings, Numa Pompilius went in the night by himself into a sacred grove to listen to the wisdom of a nymph called Aegeria. He unfolded his policies according to her advice. But she was not known to appear in Rome itself; she was the unseen influence behind the throne and her holy place was in the forest. At the same time, it must be remembered that in the oracles of the pagan world it was women who transmitted the messages from the gods. They were not young, romantic women, but old and ugly, and were only allowed to proclaim their messages through male priests, who transformed them into poetry. In the version given in Selma Lagerlöf's *Christmas Legends*, the oracle takes the form of an old woman who appears at the Capitol of Rome to warn Caesar, who is about to declare himself divine, that the Heaven-sent Saviour is already appearing on Earth and is welcomed by the shepherds. In this age inspiration was sought from the gods and women were important messengers. As long as this was so, goddesses were as much needed as gods—and so were their messengers. In the mythology of Ireland, for example, the interplay between the male god and the female goddess inspired deeds on Earth.

In the events described in the New Testament, the circle of the Apostles is composed of 12 men who followed Jesus Christ. The figure of Mary had come forth with the event of the Resurrection, becoming the guardian of the Holy Spirit, of that which descends at Whitsuntide.[3] In the history of Christianity, a process is indicated through which Mary comes to express the soul of the universe. The problem of the generations for Mary as the human mother is difficult to solve. It takes on a different aspect if it begins with the coronation instituted by Christ in the heavens, after the event of Golgotha. The original Mary is a goddess, brought down to Earth in that event which can be described as the door of Heaven opening. Christ descended to the realm of the Earth and, as His vessel, the Child Jesus was born. The goddess, who imparted soul qualities to the mother, came down with Him. But she could only stay for a short time. Thus, as she took part in the drama of Christ becoming Jesus, the human mother received the inspiration and the soul quality of the Soul of the World, which had lived in her when she accompanied the souls of the Apostles after the descent of the Holy Spirit. She became part of the event in which the community of Christians on Earth became the vessel of inspiration. The priests of the early Church were guided by the presence of the Holy Spirit, living as a goddess among men. The woman in their presence, as an inspiring goddess, could not have been with them without the gift sent by God. The Holy Spirit has come to inspire the soul of humanity, and she—Mary, who has received the Holy Spirit—is protected in the holy place (such as the sanctuary said to have been given to Her at Ephesus). She has spoken through the Apostles. She can speak in the Christian Church and, just as the gods spoke through the women in the old oracles, so in later times the Holy Spirit speaks through other chosen people, the saints.

In Christian tradition, the worship of Mary has its own history. In the National Gallery in London, the history of Mary can be followed quite clearly. In the earliest paintings, the Madonna is the Queen of Heaven. Later she is the magnificent Mother. Still later, she has left the heavenly throne and come down to Earth as the best of womankind, where she is found again in the stable with the Holy Child. In all these portrayals she is still to be worshipped by shepherds and kings, even by crowds. Finally, in the painting called *The Madonna of the Rocks* by Leonardo Da Vinci, the Madonna has gone underground, the attendant angel with her. The Mystery is sheltered below the surface of the earth. Is the Mother of God less divine below the ground than she was in the heavens? Can one not see that the Queen of Heaven is carrying her divine presence down to Earth and under the earth. Is not the dead body of Jesus Christ laid into the grave by two priestly companions, Nicodemus and Joseph of Arimathaea? Is not salvation brought about by the will of God, expressed in the depths of the fallen Earth?

In Ephesus there is to this day a house where Mary is said to have lived under the care of John, when he became bishop of that region. The tradition is based upon a vision seen by a later saint, Teresa von Konnersreuth. In the background to the picture of Mary at the foundation of Christianity, among the seven Churches quoted in the Book of Revelations, stands the figure of a goddess of pre-Christian times, Diana. From the world beyond the Earth, Diana carried down to her priests knowledge of the cosmological Being out of whom the human self descended to Earth. She gave instructions on how to preserve the relationship of the human soul in the earthly world to its origin in the heavens. Once there had been the worship of divine beings, of gods and goddesses, who became the messengers of Heaven to the Earth. Among the chosen people, the Jews, there was one messenger of God, Jehovah, who had worked with the spiritual forces of the Moon and guided his prophets, beginning with Moses. He had formulated laws for the right behaviour of people on Earth. In other religions in the ancient world there were many messengers, many gods and goddesses. All had real functions and came to give divine direction to human affairs on Earth. They belong to the time when history was made through messages from the will of God arriving on Earth, where people had begun to desire that their own will should prevail in spite of the intentions of God. Once the tension had come into being between divine and human will, messengers of the divine will had begun to be recognized.

One of the ancient stories that have been handed down and are still widely known today is the one about Cinderella. In the course of time this story has been transformed; it began long ago in ancient Egypt, when it was a story about the will of God being shared with human will.[4] It goes back to the time when slavery was a natural part of society. The characters in the original are a group of women slaves, without any choice in their way of life. They had been protected in the household of their owner. But their owner becomes old and needy and they are sent out to the market. At the sale they attract the attention of a merchant. Although he is rich and successful, his family affairs are sad. His beloved daughter has died and gone to Hades, whence she cannot return. In her memory, the merchant takes the whole group of maidens into his care and becomes their owner. The will of the gods has taken the maiden daughter and the merchant has decided to care for the whole group. Their entire destiny is redirected by the will of a human being. The gods behold this event. The problem is then laid out in a picture of how a human decision and a divine one are to be related.

In paintings found in old Egyptian tombs, the symbolic picture often used for the human being is that of the sandals or the shoes. This enters the story of the Egyptian Cinderella. While the maidens are playing beside a pool, the god Horus sends messengers to steal away a shoe of the leading maiden. The shoe is then sent by the messenger of Horus to the Pharaoh, who is discussing the events of Egypt with his counsellors. Once the symbol has arrived there is no further discussion. The Pharaoh's messengers are sent throughout the land to find which maiden the shoe belongs to, as she has the one with which it can be paired. When the maiden has been found in the garden of her protector, she must travel with his servants to the Pharaoh's throne and become his Queen and fellow ruler. Human beings have to accept that they require two feet to walk upon, two hands to undertake action. Their active will is twofold. The gods have recognized twofoldness as necessary to human beings for work on the Earth. The theme of the story describes the process through which the gods have gradually handed over to man decisions that had once been theirs alone.

This theme is illustrated further in the story of the siege of Troy (the *Iliad*). The leaders of the Greeks and the Trojans confer about their plans for winning the war. But other conferences are described, held among the gods, about which plan and which heroes to support. The outcome depends upon divine decision. Still later, certain customs prevailed, such as those at the athletic contests at Olympia. After the athletes prepared themselves, they had to pass by the statue of the goddess of victory on the way to the contests. However carefully the champions were trained, the goddess of victory was the one who decided who would win. In the course of time down the ages, decisions have passed more and more into the hands of the people. The gods have withdrawn, become obscured. Inspiration is still required, but inspired human souls have become more and more distinct from those without inspiration. Human souls who have been divine messengers have spoken to human hearers, who have then acted on the inspiration. How often in the stories of the saints have the feminine ones been the inspirers of those who performed deeds. In fact, women in the past have been inspirers rather than performers in the Sacraments. They have been more in charge of feeling and less of doing. The holiness in the soul life was renewed for humanity when the World Soul descended into the heart of the mother when the Child Jesus was born in Bethlehem. The saints have worked with the after-effect of that which inspired the soul of Mary, who held the dead body of Jesus in her arms, and came into the care of the Apostle John according to the instruction given from the Cross.

As a powerful influence in the history of the Church, especially after the first three centuries, the saints became part of its organization. In later times there was a special procedure for their appointment. A kind of lawsuit was held (and is still held) in which an advocate of the Devil has to speak before they can be appointed. Although saints are earthly people, their most suitable place has become Heaven in the life after death, rather than the present-day world. With Bernadette, there was a moment of great pressure when she was persuaded to enter a convent, because sainthood was held to be unsuitable for ordinary life on Earth. Bernadette reluctantly accepted this and later became convinced that the life after death was more suitable for her sainthood. In fact, saints are usually appointed after they have left the Earth. For them, there appears to be a need to return to the gods from whom they came to fulfil their mission as saints. They can appear in visions, as indeed the Virgin Mary is said to do. How does it come about that women have been acceptable as saints, but not as priests?

At the beginning of the Book of Revelations (Chapter 1: 17–18), the risen Christ says to John: 'I died and behold I am alive for ever more and I have the keys of death and Hades.' She who shared the Mystery of the descent is lifted up in the Resurrection and becomes the companion of the Apostles at Whitsuntide. At this moment the Holy Spirit is born and the spiritual being of Mary is raised, becoming the inspiring being of the community of Christians on Earth. She is raised to be Queen of Heaven, because she inspires an inner knowledge of the descent and ascent of the Son of God, who became the Son of Man. All the saints who have revealed in themselves how Heaven can come to Earth in human souls have become human witnesses to the gift of God, which inspires the ascent of Man. The saints bear witness to the fact that heavenly inspiration is a reality on Earth.

When the impulse for the Reformation intervened, what belonged to the heavens was brought down to Earth. All that we read of in the Gospels has been transformed into the history of people who became models of good human behaviour. It is as if all those characters in whom the divine was revealed became onlookers at human history. Saints were withdrawn into the heavens at death, to be preserved in their sainthood.

One of the objections of those who have encountered reincarnation as a part of Christianity arises from the fear that if the saints came back to Earth they would lose their sainthood. What has been achieved on Earth, they argue, needs to be preserved in Heaven. When the door of Heaven opens, in the manner promised in the Book of Revelations, it would, in this sense, show what has been preserved from the past. But this is not the meaning given to that event by St John. Streaming towards him through the door are new inspirations for the future. What happens to the veneration of Mary? It turns the inner eye of the human soul back to the beginning of things, back to the creation of man out of the heavenly forces, to the original innocence reflected even today in every newborn child. Man is intended to walk the way of history, looking ahead. He may regret what is lost, but he goes on to what is to come. Christ's descent from the heavens to the Earth gave man the power to progress without reverting to the starting point. On the other hand a splendid vision inspires the worship of Mary. As the word 'Virgin' was added to her title, it takes the mind back to the human soul before it left the heavens. It provides not a name but a memory. When the first Christians said to those around them, 'We are those on the way', they did not mean turning back, but going on.

The veneration of the Madonna has never expressed itself in the priesthood of women, for the reason that it signifies enthusiasm for a beautiful memory. Christianity is an evolving reality, requiring new intentions, and it is in this sphere of existence that the matter of the priesthood of women belongs. What is it developing in the inner life of us all today that makes it a question needing an immediate answer? Our minds can be uplifted by looking back at the image of man emerging from the heavens. How much real goodness and capacity for awe lives in the modern personality?

How creative is the sense of shame which rises in the heart of someone who regrets what he has made of himself in his earthly nature? How valuable can such regrets become in the soul which knows shame as they live on in the life after death? Regrets can induce useless despair, but they can also lead to veneration of the ideal that was not achieved. The longing for what has been lost may even be connected with visions of great aims to come.

3

The earliest history of the Christian Church in Britain was completed in 731 by the Venerable Bede. A little over a century before, Augustine of Canterbury came to Britain from Rome (597). Bede's history uses the Latin language as it was accessible at that time to churchmen. But this was not the true beginning of Christianity in Britain. Beside the Cathedral in Canterbury there is a smaller and older building dedicated to St Martin. He had led a movement for Christianity which did not come from Rome. Within the legends handed down to us in the ancient Celtic language of Ireland the origin of this still older Christianity is described.[5] But its history has been muddled by those who wished to represent the origin of the Christian Church in Britain as coming entirely from Rome. The evidence that supports these legends has been concealed in history books, which ignore such stories as the one translated by Lady Gregory, about the knowledge of the events of Good Friday.

This legend says quite plainly that the Druid priests were gifted with second sight. They were able from time to time to see what was taking place at a great distance from their everyday world. On the morning of Good Friday, according to this particular legend, the high king of Ireland went out into the forest attended by his Chief Druid. This king had a strange history. He had a rival for his high position with whom he had fought battles for a long time. When he had finally slain the rival king, he felt a wish for the talents which he had recognized in him before he had been overcome. The king proposed to the priests that, after his death, his rival's brain should be removed and sewn into his own skull, where he had received a deep wound. He was convinced this procedure would double the power of his own brain. In Ireland at that time, the Celtic people would readily have believed in such a procedure. As the Druid beside him described the event of the Crucifixion far away, the king became very angry. He was above all things a defender of the One who had come from the heavens to the Earth, being the King of the Sun. In his wrath he began to feel himself in the presence of the Roman soldiers who were performing that dreadful deed in the distant city of Jerusalem. In his longing to defend Jesus Christ, he mistook the trees in the forest for the soldiers in the distant place. Drawing his sword, he rushed upon them, dealing savage blows. As he did so, the old wound in his head opened up and the brain of his old rival fell out. But he was not able to survive such violence in his own body and he fell down dead beside the Druid.

This ancient Celtic legend and many of the same kind were preserved down the centuries among the people of Britain, but by that time they were not the only inhabitants. Invaders such as the Anglo–Saxons from Europe had arrived with their pagan outlook and pushed the Celtic people over to the west of Britain. These people had stories of their own. One of them was of the Church leader from Rome, St Gregory, who came across a slave market where a large number of boys had been brought whom the slavers had stolen from their homes in Britain. Moved by their youthful beauty, he had enquired about the origin of these fair-haired children. He was told they were Angles and he gave his famous answer: 'Not Angles, but angels.' When he became Pope he retained this memory and resolved to send missionaries to convert their people to Christianity. In consequence St Augustine and his followers arrived from across the English Channel. Canterbury became the centre of their work. Any visitor to the cathedral can walk a little way and will find the earlier church of the Celtic tradition named after St Martin. Owing to an enthusiastic churchman of the nineteenth century who restored the small building in the fashion of those times, it is not easy to detect its original style beneath the surface. Those writers who have rearranged the history of the Christian Church in Britain have thus found it easy to ignore the obvious evidence for their mistake.

With their original gift of second sight, the priests among the Celtic peoples of Britain were aware of events happening in the cosmos. They comprehended the cosmic nature of Christ as He came down to Earth. They saw Him as the King of the Sun, leaving His throne in the heavens to take up on behalf of mankind the destiny of the Earth. Being aware of the Company of Heaven, divine and real, they knew how to receive Him who came from the Sun in the strange world of the far country. They felt that the gods who worked in the heavens above would be hard to recognize in the Earth below. There is an earlier story about an Apollo-like god who, looking down upon the Earth from the heavens, explained to the goddess beside him that if he went Earthward she would find him again as a beggar. This is a scene from Celtic mythology, but it is in line with those from the Gospels, in which one can experience how difficult it was for the people on Earth to recognize the true, divine nature of Jesus Christ when He walked the roads of the Holy Land.

In the stories told by the Venerable Bede about the early life of the Christian Church in Britain there are passages dwelling entirely upon the influence of the great ladies in the Church. Their status was usually that of Abbess, that is to say, head of a convent of nuns. They were powerful in the religious life. In those early times, the social patterns in the Church accorded with the social patterns in outer life. An Abbess, or head of a convent, would have been someone who, outside the Church, would have ruled over a castle and an aristocratic family. If a landowner gave land and support for a convent, a member of his family would speedily become its head. The Abbess was also the lady of the manor, spreading her authority through the surrounding area. It was often a custom for those who had experienced earthly greatness to retire in later life into a monastic community, preparing themselves for heavenly existence after death, where perhaps they would qualify for the status belonging to aristocrats on Earth.

Many of the ladies who occupied the position of Abbess in those early times were great characters in their own right and worthy leaders of the community of the convent. Their advice and help was frequently sought by the masculine leaders of Church affairs. Such was the Abbess Hilda, who reigned in the Yorkshire area around Whitby. It is said of her that all the bishops of the North made frequent visits to her convent. She and others like her were inspired leaders, not only in theology but in the arts and the form of culture which their circumstances allowed. Of one it is said that she held large supper parties at which every guest was required to present stories from the Bible, with songs and comments suitable to their abilities. One of her household was the cowherd, Caedmon, who loved his creatures, but was not articulate in thought and speech. Terrified by the requirements of the Abbess, he ran away from the table and hid among the cows rather than make his contribution. He had a visionary dream of an angel, who instructed him in the art of telling a story and reciting poetry as required by the Abbess. When he came at last to declaim what he had heard from the angel, he produced one of the best and earliest-known poems about the creation of the world. The Abbess promoted him into a place in the convent where he could develop his creative ability for theology. None of these ladies became priests, and yet they brought inspiration out of the heavenly sphere into the earthly one. It would be fair to assume that life in their communities was more interesting and inspiring than in many of the communities of monks. Why was it that in matters of the priesthood no status or authority was given to these ladies? Perhaps something came about like the following.

A very famous story appeared in northern France in the early Middle Ages. It was about Abélard, the leading thinker and theologian of this time, and Héloïse, the beautiful and accomplished young niece of Canon Fulbert of Notre Dame. This story has been presented with the emphasis on the problem of love and marriage which so much involved them. Because of this, a very important element in their history is overlooked. At the beginning of this story Héloïse was his pupil and all her later life consulted him on questions of theology and philosophy. Socially their union, from which a son was born, was a cause of disturbance. Héloïse's uncle made a terrible physical attack on Abélard which led to him entering a monastery and she a convent. In their later life they had an interesting correspondence on theological questions. Interesting as their romance may be to modern people, it would be a pity to overlook the remarkable efficiency and leadership shown by Héloïse as Abbess of her convent. Modestly, she referred to the great intellectual abilities of Abélard. But their correspondence shows her remarkable prowess in action. Abélard maintained that every human being has a mind of his own and should think for himself. He was a pioneer before his time and opponents tried to suppress his career. His fame has outlasted that of all other great churchmen of his time. In all his problems he had the support of Héloïse, who belonged to the future in that she could splendidly carry out the aims which she grasped in thought. Before it was customary, she forged a career for herself in the Church.

The history of these two souls marks the beginning of a new period. Up to that time, the Church carried responsibility for all education, learning and art. It fostered talent and made room for new philosophies. It even adapted to the new development favoured by Abélard. Instead of instructing pupils in what was considered the right theology, the pupils began to find their own way with the help of disputation. Theologians travelled from monastery to monastery, taking with them new concepts, which could be set up in dispute against the old ones. The skilful handling of thought became the means of defending new propositions. Abélard himself is reported as saying that he valued the thoughts in disputation more than the trophies of battle. So it came about that, through the Middle Ages, the power of the mind to handle various nuances of thought developed in disputation and the capacity of the mind to think for itself increased. The Church was as much responsible for this as it was for inner gifts and endeavours. In the pursuit of theology, under the care of the Church, mental abilities developed and became established. But then a shadow loomed. Fearful about what was right and proper in religious thought, the Church established the Inquisition. As the human mind became more capable in thought, so there arose to meet it the anxiety that true and right thoughts must fight with the wrong for the honour of the truth.

At that time it was not possible to imagine that learning by error might be a way to truth. There was no experience of the extent to which experiments in thought could lead to the discovery of higher verities. Instead, it was imagined that erroneous thought would lead the soul down to Hell. It was even believed that the earthly fires that burnt the heretics would save the soul from the everlasting flames of Hell, and was therefore a blessing for evil-doers and wrong-believers. But the persecutions of those times cast their shadow over the newly discovered power of individual thinking. All through those early centuries there was a continual conflict between thinking and the fear it aroused. There was also an opposition between the masculine and feminine picture of the human being. The man expected of himself valorous deeds, whether as a fighter or a thinker. An old Celtic poem described the fate of the warriors (*Godgoddin*): 'The warriors arose together, together they met, together they attacked with single purpose. Short were their lives, long mourning left to their kinsmen ... I have lost too many of my kinsmen, of three hundred champions who set out, only one would come back.' What then was required of the women? They had to bear mourning and grief, but they were also required to inspire. In the literature of the time, songs and tales tell of the men who gathered their strength to fight, through love and devotion to a lady as distant and unknown as a goddess. For a long while the female element was looked upon as goddess-like, as the old Celts had done. One of the Celtic poems is about an invitation to the land of women, which is also the earthly paradise. At the end of the poem it says: 'Then the woman went from them and they did not know where she went.' She had come to call them from the place of battles and fighting to a land of peace, of loveliness. Such, in a very few words, was the message women brought to meet the sturdy will to fight of the men. In another sense, one might say that in these old myths and legends the will of the warrior was the role of the man and the singing of peace and happiness that of the woman. When Abélard the thinker wrote to Héloïse, his former wife, about her leadership of the nuns, the element of will had begun to arise on the female side and, from the male, there came the sense of direction. It was a prophecy of change.

4

The strongest factor in the making of history is the changing human consciousness.[7] In museums, in which the customs at different times are recorded, there is little evidence of the changes in heart and mind, unless the viewer looks for them himself. There is a large country house in Worcestershire, the Commanderie, in the park of which a battle of Royalists and Roundheads took place in the time of Cromwell. The house used to be a museum, open to the public. In the fireplace of the entrance hall one could see two pairs of boots, which had been found in the park. One pair came from the army of Roundheads. The boots were strong and plain, the toes square, the heels low. One could well picture the soldier who owned them having been a farm worker and used to plodding about his fields. The other pair clearly came from the army of the Royalists. The Roundheads used to cut their hair short to fit under their helmets. It is said that their method of hair cutting was very simple, a pudding basin being turned upside down on the head and the hair cut off round it. The Royalists wore long curls falling over their lace collars. Their boots had pointed toes and high heels and would have looked fine on the rider of a horse, with sword slung beside him. As a matter of course the conversation which would have belonged to one pair of boots would have been different from the other. These boots showed two different kinds of consciousness coming into conflict in the course of time.

At each stage of consciousness in history, the relationship between male and female has been different. In the childhood of mankind, in the Garden of Paradise, as it is represented in the Bible, the original oneness of the human being was known. But the Devil, in the form of the serpent, was allowed into Paradise. On the tree in which he installed himself, the fruit grew which could change human consciousness into an intelligent one and the human will into an arbitrary one. It is clear that this change was necessary so that man might become active on Earth. The closing of the Gate of Heaven was inevitable. But that which is described in the Book of Genesis is a hasty and unprepared development. To produce the consequences so clearly described in the Bible, the interference of the serpent was necessary.

The first act of the serpent was to separate Eve from Adam and at the same time make them dependent on each other. The serpent offered the apple, which was the symbol of the change in consciousness from dependence on their surroundings to the condition of exerting their own will. Eve accepted the apple from the serpent and Adam accepted it from her. In the immediate consciousness of each other, they were estranged from the divine presence, which appeared to them in the cool of the evening, and thus they had to experience a new awareness of themselves and their nakedness. When the angel with the flaming sword drove them into another existence, human souls became divided in their nature. Partly they would live in the heavens, directed by the divine will of heavenly being. But the gate of birth enabled them to descend for a while into independent life on Earth, returning to the heavens again through the gate of death. To be born on Earth required two parents, one with male qualities and one with female. But the individual person would confront death on his own. Nowadays, where relationships are so confused, little children still make it quite clear that they expect to live with two parents, although each will find his own deathbed. For the young child, the motherly element is that which leads him down to Earth, being protected through the early years until entry into full life on the Earth. The fatherly element shows the child the capacities that he will develop, until he also unfolds his individual will in deeds on Earth. In grown-up life, the female element often continues to represent the cosmic forces which are heavenly; the masculine element represents that which, willingly, uses and calls upon the forces of the Earth.

Naturally enough this is a generalization, best understood by little children, who know instinctively what kind of help they expect from the mother and the father. But this too passes through changes of consciousness in the course of history. The English king James I was placed by his heredity in an awkward position. His mother was Mary Queen of Scots, but his throne was inherited from Queen Elizabeth I who, to protect her position, rightly or wrongly ordered the beheading of Mary. In Westminster Abbey there are two side chapels behind the altar, erected by James I. One is dedicated, with a statue, to his mother, the other is dedicated, with a statue, to the queen from whom he took the throne. He had wished to show equal respect to both. In reality, they represented very different types of consciousness. Mary had awakened mystical reverence and worship in her presence and had followed, in her ordinary character, the feminine longing for husband and motherhood. Elizabeth, by contrast, behaved as a higher being and built up the character of a queen with divine rights. The royal processions were memories of ancient ones, which accompanied gods on Earth. Her robes and crowns were remarkable for their more-than-earthly splendour and she was not to be expected to walk on the bare ground, which those courtiers like Sir Walter Raleigh recognized by throwing their cloaks under her feet. But she showed more earthly intelligence than the more mystical Mary and made fewer mistakes. She was ready to be wooed, but she never descended to an earthly marriage, nor to motherhood. She became known as the Virgin Queen and demonstrated how very cleverly she had chosen her style of reigning. She had courtiers and wooers enough, but she remained as unattainable as a goddess. In her image, the woman capable on Earth was still the shadow of the one who reigned by divine right.

The far-reaching problem of the interaction between human will and divine will has descended into history step by step since Egyptian times. Gradually, human nature has evolved the capacity to exercise will on Earth, but man is still an unfinished product of the universe even though he is no longer so dependent on guidance from beyond himself. The feminine capacities are now much less differentiated from the masculine ones. Something has taken place that makes the modern man or woman more able to transcend distinctions of gender. It is acceptable nowadays to recognize that masculine and feminine characteristics constitute two parts of a whole and that both these parts belong to each individual. Everyone has both a male and a female character, because something further has become established on Earth which expresses the wholeness of the human being. In terms of the philosophy introduced by Rudolf Steiner, this is the Ego. The word may be used in a different sense to describe the feeling of selfishness with which each person today feels obliged to defend his self-interest. It is, in fact, the shadow of the true reality of the higher self, which is expressed in the conscience as the organ of moral responsibility. The conscience can be an unreality if judgements are made solely out of conventions of social behaviour, or out of unthinking respect for laws. When the conscience becomes gifted with imagination, it expresses a higher purpose. This inspires the heart of the person who recognizes himself as a spiritual being on Earth, knowing that he is spiritual before birth and continues to be so after death. Previously, the individual on Earth could only express his or her spirituality in either a male or a female form. Now the spiritual element has become stronger than the form. There may still be masculine and feminine expressions for the quality of egohood. It can become will force in man and an activity of imagination in a woman, but behind both there stands the spiritual reality of the Ego. That which had been divided on Earth through the interference of the serpent can now, because the Son of God has become the Son of Man through Christ, express itself without contradiction in either form.

Egohood can produce devotion to ideals in a man or a woman equally. Whereas the man may put more forces of will at the disposal of his true self and the woman often offers more imagination in thought and feeling in her undertakings, each strives to be a true expression of the sense of responsibility produced by egohood. The important thing is the inner activity through which the action has come about. The quality of egohood expresses itself in the purpose and external execution. In the relationships formed between modern men and women, the opportunity to unfold true selfhood is present, although the expression of it may fail. In the present phase of history, it is easy to fall back on old forms, because they seem quieter and less demanding. But history makes progress, even when it brings disturbance with it. Unselfish selfhood requires more moral effort and, above all, more imagination than the conventions established in an earlier phase of history. Conscience may seem to be more concerned with the motive of behaviour than its consequences. It is a natural impulse to say 'I meant well' when wondering why the results are so different from what one intended. To establish customs of conduct means to leave the problems of selfhood out of account. To decide that one will always give something from one's purse to beggars, who are many at the present time, or to fund-raisers supporting good causes, is simply to economize on the moral effort of one's selfhood. To do nothing about it has the same effect. Decisions, large and small, bother the modern person continually, but in this way he can live up to the demands made upon him because of the time in which he lives. Egohood has now descended into daily life and produces its own heroism. Sir Philip Sydney gave an early example of this kind of heroism when, on the battlefield on which he died in 1586, he gave the water which he needed himself to an ordinary soldier whose need he thought to be greater. The example can be interpreted as an act of unselfishness, which it certainly was. But the manner in which it was performed is clearly something more: 'We are both dying in battle, we are both in need, we are both human beings with a spiritual reality treasured within us.' Such an insight is present in the action of such a hero. It acknowledges the spiritual humanity in the other. Both stand at the gate to Eternity, recognizing in each other the presence of that which comes from Eternity and returns there. It is easy to read the story in another way, but today our need is to recognize and understand how the everlasting egohood lives in another person. When we find it, the truest heroism can be identified. The fact that the emotional impulse to belittle heroism is common today makes it easy to miss the point. Sometimes a child says something beyond its own comprehension when experiencing the realities of this world. A little girl, visiting a cemetery with a small boy to put flowers on the grave of an aged neighbour, looked round at all the graves with great concern. Something moved in her heart at the memory of all the kind people they had both known, who had helped them on their way through childhood and who had turned into memories. To her the many graves had become an experience of wasted bodies, which the souls of those she loved had given up. After considering the matter, she said to the boy: 'It's all right, they come back, there is no waste.'

When someone has fulfilled all the duties and obligations that confront him in daily life, he can sometimes ask himself whether he has done all that can be expected of him, or whether there is still more to fulfil. He may wonder: is this all I am living for? Then he may resolve upon another kind of action which he wishes to freely carry out. There was once a modern poet, known as Stevie Smith,[8] who died not long ago. She lived a modest life in a London suburb, carrying out her duties at home to mother and sister and enjoying the company of an aunt, who had decided to join them because the usual obligations of the father were not being fulfilled. She was faithful to her task in life until her retirement, but was much moved in her heart and mind beyond the needs of these circumstances. She had many opportunities to marry, but every time she met a possible husband—and it happened quite often—she foresaw obligations that would have destroyed the pattern of life in which her poems could be created. She exemplifies the woman of today who decides for herself what she will do with her time and strength. It was not exactly a conflict between marriage and career. It was more a problem of how she would live if she accepted any of the men as a husband, for her circumstances would then be arranged by someone to whom the poems did not seem a necessary or urgent task. Her poetry did not seem to be a duty, but an expression of that in her which lived beyond obligation. She expressed the experiences that her way of living offered to her, but in a manner that revealed the eternal realities behind earthly forms.

In writing about herself, Stevie Smith has described the situation of every modern person, whether male or female. What kind of pattern shall I produce in my life? What earthly obligations need I fulfil? Must I accept everything that is thrust upon me? How one answers such questions are one's own responsibility, because most traditional obligations are no longer acceptable. The most important question is what to do next with oneself. Very few can foresee how they will live some years ahead. New liberties bring new uncertainties and everyone will find his or her own way of expressing these dilemmas. One psychiatrist said recently that most of his patients had not known how to be born in the present age. In other words, they are facing questions that they cannot answer. One reason for quoting Stevie Smith is the direct way in which she stated her own answer. We have many more liberties than our ancestors, even in one generation, but can we face the risks?

5

In nature, after a tree has come into blossom the process of fading produces a new fruit. In the course of history an analagous process is not so plain, because the moral forces in the human soul are involved. In this sense, the Fall of Man from the innocence of Paradise was a negative process, yet without it no development towards responsibility would have come about. The father of Henry James is reported to have told his son that the best thing Eve ever did for Adam was to get him thrown out of Paradise. By this he must have meant that the innocence of early childhood, if it is not relinquished in the process of growing up, turns into stupidity. The theme was explored by Goldsmith in *The Vicar of Wakefield*. The consciousness of the human soul has changed in the process of becoming aware of evil as well as of good, giving rise to the discovery of compassion and forgiveness. Our involvement with this inner process brings about the means of handling them and developing the inner power of responsibility within oneself. Mary, crowned by the Son of God as the Queen of Heaven, has had the special charm that inspires the worship of the divine out of which human souls have been born. If this is cherished as the privilege of the Mother, it will not evolve into 'ego-consciousness'.

Within the pictures of the Gospels there is a picture of another Mary, called Magdalene. In the Gospel of St Luke, Chapter 8, she appears among the characters around Jesus Christ. At the feast in the Pharisee's house, she is said to have intruded at a reception given in honour of Jesus Christ (Luke, Chapter 7, v. 37). She is called a sinner and represented as a prostitute. She performed a holy act, not by invitation, but as an intruder. She washed the feet of Jesus Christ with her tears, wiped them with her hair, kissed them and anointed them with an ointment that she had brought with her. The host protested, but the answer given by Jesus Christ is quoted in the Gospel (v. 47): 'Her sins, which are many, are forgiven, for she loved much, but he who is forgiven little loves little.' And he said to her: 'Your sins are forgiven,' and added: 'Your faith has saved you, go in peace.' A scene of the same nature is described in the Gospel of St Mark (Chapter 14) as taking place just before the Last Supper, near the end of the life on Earth of Jesus Christ. The host is not a Pharisee but a leper who has been cured, and the anointing with the ointment takes place on the head. The complaint made by those present is not against the woman herself, but against the extravagance of the gesture. The standards cultivated by the people around were that money should be given in charity to the poor, but Jesus Christ described the gesture of the woman as a ritual for the burial of His body when He died. Another version of this event is found in the Gospel of St John, Chapter 12. The invitation is given by Lazarus after he had been restored to life, the supper is prepared by Martha, and the ointment is offered by Mary. The objection is made by Judas Iscariot, who estimates everything in terms of money. It seems in this description as if the woman who was a sinner is also Mary, the sister of Martha, the doer of good deeds. Many readers of the Bible have solved this problem in their own way. Are we to imagine that the most inward-looking of the friends of Jesus Christ and the best of His listeners was the one who had earlier expended her devotion in the practice of prostitution. So great a change-round is possible and often found in the lives of the saints. But the mystery becomes greater when one observes that the one who showed Jesus Christ the way to the tomb of Lazarus was Martha, to whom He said: 'I am the resurrection and the life.' (St John, Chapter 11, v. 25.)

The forces of the heart are transformed in Mary and those of the will in Martha. Both are made ready to serve the nature of the ego in the future existence of man. Born out of the fallen existence of mankind, they are lifted up by the emergence of active forces of goodness. Both Martha and Mary are active in love before Lazarus is raised to life, but he is born again out of death and needs a new embodiment of that which works in the heart and that which works in the will. The three together at this feast are a prophecy of what will arise in man through Christ, who has descended to the Earth in order to transform the earthly nature, making it possible to rise again. They show in themselves the true nature of egohood that rises beyond egotism. They prophesy that the ego will only truly find itself when it rises on the Earth into the power to receive and to give love. Disguised in egotism, egohood will rise again as the divine nature that has been rescued from death. The vision of the Mother with the Child shows the Heaven-endowed soul descending into the darkness of life on Earth. Born again out of death, it shines with the light of the spirit, through which death is overcome. Lazarus represents the ego rising up, to be given by Martha and Mary the new forces of heart and mind through which man will become reborn through resurrection.

In the stories from the Gospels there is first described that which will be the consequences of the death and resurrection of Christ Himself on Golgotha. In terms of earthly logic the consequences are worked out before the deed itself is represented. Those who were witnesses were shown the purpose of the event in advance of its happening. Could they have understood such new knowledge, the disciples would not have fallen asleep in the Garden of Gethsemane. The way in which light and darkness interchanged as the event of Golgotha unfolded was more confusing than the hearts of the Apostles could bear. They fell asleep when they should have been awake. They bequeathed to those who came after them a struggle for understanding and wakefulness. That which could not happen at the time, because of their weakness, became the task of those who follow. When the disciples later on founded the first Church of Christians, they proclaimed themselves to be witnesses who had been present and therefore knew. Those to whom they spoke were able to accept this through the light of their faith. The gift of the Holy Spirit awakened in the Apostles the real experience through which they had slept. Thereby they became witnesses to that which they had not known, and the light of the spirit in the people around them enabled them to become witnesses to the awakening in the hearts of the Apostles. The Christian Church was founded on a great event of awakening. The Apostles and the people with them awakened to the Mystery of Golgotha, until they could all bear witness to what they could see and know.

Through thinking, it is possible to understand the value and importance of an event after it has happened. So much of the mind's capacity is called 'reflection' in truth. Reflection and understanding can awaken the processes of will. The Christian soul can then know that resurrection has become a divine deed done on Earth, which can further the evolution of the human soul. In one sense, the Apostles slept when they should have been awake. In another, they call us, who come after them, to find through reflection a wakeful understanding of the future. They call upon us to work with them at that which is not yet fulfilled. With each development in consciousness, another quality of understanding can be achieved. We may learn from the past, but we awaken in the present to the future. The secret of the Apocalypse becomes the challenge to further awakening.

The representation of the young god supported by two goddesses is older than Christianity. The theme is frequently found in the art of ancient Egypt. It is a prophecy of that which, in the Gospels, arrived among human beings on Earth. It is a mystery, foreseen long ago, of that which was then still in the process of incarnation. It would be wise to realize that Lazarus does not simply represent someone who, dying an untimely death, was brought back to his destiny on Earth. He has become the representative of man on Earth who was called upon to visit the spiritual world and bring down to the Earth certain forces out of which man's evolution can proceed. If the Egyptian pictures are taken seriously, they portray a heavenly treasure for mankind which had not yet come to Earth. Jesus Christ brought Lazarus out of the tomb to bring this treasure to us. In the overcoming of death on the Cross, Christ Himself saved for the Earth that which had been bestowed upon Lazarus by the heavenly powers. The two sisters could supply, in their purity, forces of mind and heart by which the new treasure could become effective for everyone who carries the burden of responsibility here. A picture arises of the male will supported and given expression by that which comes from each side through the two sisters. If one looks into the present and the future, one can see the picture changing. The human character becomes a unity in which all three have come together. The ego-will is supported in the individual by the heart forces from one side and by the understanding mind from the other. Nowadays, each individual can expect to find all three within himself and recognizes these soul qualities in another person. A picture can thus emerge of what the arrival of ego consciousness in our earthly life can mean. Lazarus, Martha and Mary unite in the mind and heart of everyone who allows the transformation to happen. Earlier, these qualities were sought and manifested in different people and the unity was found in relationships between them. But gradually the time has come when they have become one. It can therefore be understood how it comes about that the distinction between man and woman is changing. In terms of outer dress, it is becoming more difficult to distinguish the two in their appearance. Today, trousers are the fashion, but this may well change. Flowing garments might well become the vogue, but it is unlikely that garments supporting the distinction will come to the fore.

Lazarus can become the figure through whom priesthood is seen to become a reality in the Christian Church. In the past the priest was supported by forces carried by female figures, through whose influence the priestly character could become active. But in modern times, in the psychological experience of many people, the three soul forces have become absorbed into the individual, endowing women with the same faculties as were once associated with men. Women are now eager to perform all the former male functions. One of the problems produced by this is that, when women have done the work once done by men, they wish in their spare time to be women again. In terms of this development of egohood, there is no longer any reasonable cause for women not becoming priests. In fact, most of the arguments against the priesthood of women arise out of conditions in the past and are tinged with personal prejudice. Since the Christian Community is a modern form of Christianity, arguments based on the past are inappropriate. It is not a form of conflict which haunts the Christian Community. Quite another question arises when another experience enters practical life. One may ask what effect this new development has on the actual work of the Christian Community.

6

In the Christian Community, which is the newest and most recent church in the history of Christianity, the priest has a threefold task. The first one is the celebration of the sacraments. They are now seven, which belong to the experience of man as he travels between birth and death. Since the first community of Christians became a reality on the first Sunday of Whitsuntide, there have been arguments about the nature of the sacraments and how many there are. Now it is realistic to restore the concept of the number seven, through which an individual finds his earthly life consecrated. They are deeds of will, reflecting the inspirations of the angels, archangels and all the company of Heaven. The sacraments are actions performed on Earth which unite with activities in the heavens. They fulfil the promise which Jacob saw in his dream, when the ladder was set up between the two worlds.[9] The priest undertakes to give his forces of will to actions and words on Earth that are then received in the heavens. Such deeds are not the result of personal impulses, but are the highest expression of what is universally human.

The celebrating priest does not speak for himself, but seeks to express the spiritual nature in man himself. There are moments in ordinary life when common needs are felt. In the bustle of modern cities, when standing in a queue for transport, for instance, there is such an experience. It can affect everyone with the urge to compete. Our common need becomes a struggle of all against all. The best that our neighbours can hope for is that I go away and disappear. But in this kind of modern situation something else can happen. The neighbour may make room for me, push me up on to the bus, acknowledge that my need and his need are the same and that the experience, which pushed us into competition, may become a moment of sharing in what is the need of everyone. It can illumine the mind and heart with a concept of the nature of human need, allowing compassion to transform competition. By contrast, at the top of the ladder, need is understood and transformed into an experience of brotherhood. The sacraments are found at the top of the ladder, the need at the bottom. But if our human life on Earth is to be spiritualized, both are necessities.

There was once a hymn which perplexed schoolchildren who sang it. It was intended to raise their thoughts to brotherhood of the highest order. It began with the words: 'O brother man fold to thy heart thy brother.'[10] No one could imagine how to do something like that. If 'brother man' meant everyone, there were too many of us to make this possible. If it meant man as an abstract principle, how could he be folded into a real heart? There have been many expressions for the brotherhood of man which could not be actually realized. The communion service in the Christian Community is called the 'Act of Consecration of Man'. We all need consecration, because we have not yet reached that at which we are aiming. The spiritual idea of ourselves is still far away in the heavens, but when what is far above us is expressed in an earthly action, which everyone can recognize, it takes on reality and ceases to be abstract. Such is the purpose of the sacraments. How is the one who celebrates them to live up to this?

He has to find the sphere of the eternal soul in the midst of the multitude of impressions which make up so much of our experience. We move in Eternity whenever we know that time has not split us up into ever-changing patterns. Behind our personal selves is that which gathers from our changing experiences the substance that will be as real after death as it is now. It was also real before we were born and we shall carry it into that which we shall become. We begin in the sacraments at the bottom of the ladder. Garments called vestments are required and have to be made, but the pattern is universal. Objects are required. A cup containing water and grape juice is placed on an altar bearing seven candles in seven candlesticks, which when lighted produce seven flames. Above the altar a picture is needed that conveys the idea of Christ as the source and origin of what man is meant to become out of the struggling pilgrim he is. The picture will succeed in this aim in proportion as the artist can transcend himself. All these things require the overcoming of earthly limitations.

The celebrating priest overcomes such limitations when he is able to speak and act as an eternal soul meeting other eternal souls. The ladder is climbed and all meet in the spiritual height at the top. Why is the Act of Consecration of Man, for example, except for certain changes at the Festivals of the Christian year, continually the same? It awakens and makes evident the eternal soul within us all. Is what belongs to Eternity always the same? We know ourselves on the Earth as beings changing with time. We long for experiences. In spite of our fears, we are glad of change. We are training ourselves for awareness of Eternity. If, in attending the sacraments, similar words are heard, they change into the meanings that arise out of the depths of Eternity. The eternal soul is coming alive in the experiences which come about at the top of the ladder, where dependence on the ever-changing world around us ceases. Inner realities do not depend upon outer variety. What is necessary to release our hearts and minds for Eternity? What do we know about ourselves? How much do we depend upon likes and dislikes, pleasures and pains, wants and wishes, sympathies and antipathies? The restrictions that form the personal pattern on which so much reliance is put nowadays can be transcended. How much do they tie us up in the personal pattern we seem to have chosen for ourselves? We can rise above them.

As recently as 1971, a remarkable modern person, whom we have met earlier in these pages, finished her present destiny on Earth and died. She wrote poetry of an unusual style and the name which she chose to use was Stevie Smith. She led an ordinary life in an unremarkable suburb of London, but her perceptions were not at all ordinary. When she wrote about herself, as she was once asked to do, her writing took the form of an argument in her own mind between different aspects of her character. It seems that when she had listened to them all, another part of herself made the decisions about her destiny. One could say that she listened to the advice of the different selves at the bottom of the ladder and then followed the injunctions of a greater self at the top. As a result, everything she did was unusual. But at the close of her life she composed a poem about a meeting in a London park with the Christ of the Second Coming. She felt as if everyone in the park had met Him too and was advising Him on how to behave, in order to fulfil their own expectations. But he, according to the author, was in reality singing. Had the people round about been able to stop listening to their own expectations, they would have heard His singing and partaken in the revelation He was bringing to them. To what extent did the people in the park become able to free themselves to hear what came to meet them from the top of the ladder?

When considering what has to be overcome on the way to realization of the fact that in our time women may become priests, enabling their eternal souls to go into action, we may look at examples found in the past. An ancient distinction has long been made between Martha and Mary. It became a social custom to put women into the position of Martha, satisfying the needs of the body for the sake of human health. Where the Mary aspect has become stronger, then Mary has been incomplete without a Martha to attend upon her. Nowadays, the woman is in a position to ask herself how far she should follow Martha and how far Mary. Neither can continue without each other, so how is the balance to be achieved? People answer this question differently, according to their circumstances. But how can an answer be found which is satisfactory? Is a woman becoming a priest saying to herself, 'Am I becoming Mary and discarding Martha?' Is every woman with a profession struggling with this problem? Is it just a custom that every woman is a Martha? Can she be a Mary at the same time? Or must she choose between them?

In these days of developing self-consciousness, it is not simply a question of the one or the other. In the modern world, each person, whether man or woman, must achieve a balance between the two. It is no longer the case that the world consists of Marthas and Marys, for now each person carries both. How far can one seek to resolve the problem of balance between these two? There cannot, of course, be a general rule for everyone, but it is true that human feet must walk on the ground of ordinary existence and the head, needed as it is in ordinary life, should nevertheless be able to rise above it. In the Bible it is stated that Christ spoke about the Resurrection first of all to Martha (St John, Chapter 11, v. 25). The Resurrection is a Mystery pointing to the foundation of our Earth existence.

The problem of Martha and Mary is one of reconciliation. It belongs to the life of people today to find the secret of reconciliation as a principle. It will still appear different for a man and a women under modern conditions, but the common aim will be to find reconciliation as a solution. There are enough old prejudices to cause difficulties, but they have nothing to do with solving problems.

There are other pictures of Mary and other Marys in the Gospels. There is Mary, the mother of the Child from the heavens. The fashion for believing that the father is not present has arisen out of misunderstandings about the picture of the Virgin. It continues to cause theological worry. The worship of Mary as such causes her to become a goddess, who never touches the Earth in the true sense. In contrast, there is another figure in the Gospels, Mary Magdalene, the one who has descended too far, who has become involved with the machinations of temptation, turning into self-indulgence. But for whom? Each one in modern times is facing a problem of his own, when he sees the twofold picture, the goddess who uplifts and the one who pulls down. What does one admire? What is one willing to worship? Who is to blame but oneself? Who is one to admire in making choices? What does it mean that Christ Himself has refused to condemn and brought into human life on Earth the power of forgiveness? How can that itself be understood?

The eternal soul carries within itself the courage to take the problems of human history into its own being. The problems of being human have been solved by Christ, as He descended from the world of the heavens to that of man on Earth. From the top of the ladder to the bottom, He shed His light. Where His light shines, where His voice is heard, the problems change. At the Cross on Golgotha, Mary, the mother, and Mary Magdalene stood together. Both have their place in the history of human evolution and in both Christ works as a reality in the process of man's resurrection. Mary Magdalene was the first to meet the risen Christ and to speak of Him to the others. Certainly it was Thomas who asked the most profound of the questions, but through Mary the questions first arose. The Mystery itself arises through the meeting of Mary and Thomas, but the answer is carried into the hearts of each one of the Apostles and the women, according to his or her own faith.

7

The second task of the priest in the Christian Community is to share in developing the further understanding of Christianity. Those who find confidence in the teachings of Rudolf Steiner will be aware of his statement that Christianity came into the world from the heavens for a cosmic purpose, but at a time when it could not be understood. The thoughts and deeds of Jesus Christ recorded in the Gospels are still not truly understood. Those who experienced what happened in the short time He lived on Earth had no means of understanding the events to which they bore witness. There is a parallel in what has happened in the history of Christianity with what is experienced in a person's own lifetime: the event comes first and the understanding later. Down the centuries, since the event from which we count our years in time, great efforts of understanding have been made, some of them rightly famous. But the process by which we estimate our means of understanding is not yet finished. Christ has brought from the heavens to the Earth spiritual forces that have changed the history of mankind, that bring a living future into our consciousness. But the task is unfinished. It is an interesting study to follow how the religious impulse in human hearts manifests itself.

Widespread in the souls of people, even today, is the feeling that one is not what one was meant to be. Disappointment with oneself is the commonest of human problems. It is a sign of weakness to find other people who can be blamed for this state of affairs. In the last resort, among people who know the Bible, this can be blamed on the expulsion from Paradise. In a sense this experience of unfulfilment belongs to every human being. Growing out of the innocent period of early childhood, the dawning awareness of something wrong in human nature is known to everyone. In earlier ages, great undertakings were promoted out of a much more intense longing for Paradise than is found nowadays. The belief that somewhere on Earth Paradise could be found still existed. Those who knew the sea coast, especially among the Celtic peoples, were convinced that somewhere there was an island where the conditions of Paradise still prevailed. The mighty voyage of the Irish saint called Brendan[11] is an example of this longing. He set out with his disciples in a fragile boat to find this land where people of unspoilt nature still lived. He reached the coast of Florida and was one of the earlier discoverers of America. But what happened to end the story? Out of the forest near the shore a mysterious figure came to meet him. He might have been a priest of a hidden temple, or an angel of Paradise. He said to St Brendan, with a conviction that could not be withstood: 'Go back to the land you left, the time is not ripe. You must not remain.' Without argument, Brendan and his disciples went back to their ship. When they arrived home, so much time had passed that they had all become old men, unrecognizable to those who came to meet them. Had they in fact been in Paradise? They themselves did not really know, but they had learnt that it was not for them.

The longing for a lost paradise can always rise up again, even in modern people, and is still an inspiration in a number of religions. But through Christianity another ideal has entered the religious life. At the end of the Bible, in the Book of Revelations, the evolving history of mankind is described as a journey onwards into the future. The way onwards is a much more strenuous undertaking than the way back, but it is the essence of Christianity. Ever since the Resurrection of Christ the way has been open for mankind, and He Himself has become the Leader of the Way and the Leader on the Way. What such a simple statement means has still to be understood, especially in our own time. The whole history of man is involved. It is the particular task of a new movement in Christianity to take up and continue the new ideas and thoughts which become possible for our generation. Such a huge task is to be shared by many people, requiring the thinking of many minds. It is not confined to one generation, but needs to be continually passed on for the sake of the wisdom streaming from the future. As it is undertaken, Christianity itself becomes more real and more forceful as it becomes more and more understood. What we know we become. We should avoid the modern error, which persuades us that we are merely onlookers at external processes. Thinking, feeling and willing in the human soul are involved in the process of knowledge; understanding is a process of becoming and creates in man his future destiny.

In an undertaking of such proportions, a careful approach is required. The feminine gift of imagination is to be absorbed into the process, as much as the more masculine qualities of the intellect. Nowadays this is easily recognized in many areas of life. In fact, it can sometimes be argued that the feminine mind grasps new ideas more quickly than the masculine. As in many other areas, opposites are the better for being reconciled and not for being removed. Can there be any reason why sermons should not be preached by women just as much as men? Can there be any reason why theology should not be advanced by women's minds as well as men's? Is there, in fact, any reason, except that it means a change in old customs? What emerges today as the most important factor in our human life is the strength of the individuality to balance out the inequalities that were so important in the past. And what is most valuable to the individuality is such a state of awareness that the three forces of the soul—thinking, feeling and willing—should be recognized, understood and summoned to act in useful proportions. It might be objected that this requires a development in psychology. In our time it would be more realistic to look beyond the distinction of male and female to the selfhood which is common to all. It is tiresome at times not to be able to decide whether to refer to the human self as he, she or it. But the exercise of deciding is valuable. It calls upon the mind to transcend the distinctions of sex in practice and to deal with the greater realities. The human being can then be recognized as a much bigger entity than that of which we are usually aware in daily life.

What does it mean to be human? Each of us is a changing person. Each of us goes in his different way through the changing rhythms of a lifetime. The child is human, the youth is human, the grown-up person also, who will become middle-aged and finally an old man or woman. As Rudolf Steiner has pointed out, we assume this to be a fact, without accepting the consequences of this idea. Christianity has no different rules for men and women, or children and grown-ups. There are no differences of nation or race. It relates to what is common to us all: the life before birth, the entry into Earth existence, the journey towards the gate of death and the return to the heavens, from which the soul has descended. Such a great reality of human experience leads us to imagine how Christ Himself saw mankind. He is said to have seen with compassion—compassion for human souls, who never feel quite at home in the world that belongs to them; compassion for those who are struggling to become what they should be but who lose so easily what they really are; compassion for the little child, for the dashing youth, for the concerned grown-up person, and for the anxious older one. Is it not worthwhile trying to imagine the compassion of Christ, even if it means stretching our minds to a much wider view of history than we normally contemplate? Is not this a greater perspective than that which we meet in ordinary life, one to which the understanding of Christianity would call us, if we are willing to transcend the usual distinctions of class or nation or race?

An even wider perspective opens before the mind when reincarnation is admitted as a fact of life which can enter into Christianity nowadays.[12] The danger that the separate incarnation may be considered too unimportant, in view of its vast possibilities, may well be the reason why reincarnation has so long been unacceptable in the Christian religion. It is aptly illustrated in a story told in a magazine of a taxi driver in Yokohama driving an American visitor. The American is said to have remarked: 'Please drive more carefully. We only live once, you know.' To which the driver is supposed to have replied: 'You may only live once, but I have many lives and this is the least important.' Apart from this mistaken notion, the concept of repeated lives on Earth brings with it a greater picture of man. It would be a misunderstanding to believe that it means the same kind of life being repeated again and again. In reality, it is the instrument by which the single soul receives the opportunity to know more and more about the nature of mankind. In general, reincarnation means the return to Earth at a different stage of history, in a different part of the world and in the opposite sex from that of the present life. The woman of one life will tend to become the man in the next life who will thereby balance out in himself one-sided tendencies and experiences. No one, except in the most unusual circumstances, can expect to return to the same nationality. The soul is on the way to become further identified with mankind as a whole. Relationships with other people can reach a climax and become past history. Might this become an occasion for sadness? This is not at all necessary, because the consciousness of each one is expanding from personal affinities to that which makes mankind a reality for him. There is no need to lose the people we love, but there are many more people whom we shall need to love than those whom we know at present. We have the opportunity to expand and enlarge our experience as we grow in humanity.

It is particularly valuable at the present time to make a new start in religious life, because it is here that the past tends to intrude so remarkably. Travelling on a bus through the city of London, I once heard two young men returning from a wedding to which they had been invited. Having spent the afternoon in a church, they had come away with religion on their minds. One said to the other: 'I shall be all right, I don't have to think about religion any more. I was well brought up and I have my childhood faith which will last me for life.' It would have been possible to ask him whether he still had the same clothes that he wore in childhood, the same occupations, the same relationships. He would certainly have said no. But in religious matters he was content to remain a child. Such attitudes often stand between people of today and the progress they might make in Christianity. At the same time, when a new interest awakens in religion, it often begins with an enquiry into the philosophies from the world of the East and from something that is centuries old. A religion stretching into the future seems unnatural to many in our modern era. Religion belonging to the childhood of mankind, or to the child in the soul of an individual person, cannot fill the deeper need of the modern version of 'Homo religiosus', quoted by Mircea Eliades.

How can religion become alive again in the present and for the future? One can realize that history is not just a series of events flowing from the past into the present. In reality, it is a process of changing consciousness among human beings. It is made quite clear in the Gospels that Christianity began with the event of the heavens opening and the angels accompanying the Son of God towards the world of the Earth. He who carried within Himself the highest wisdom of the heavens decided to experience the God-forsaken Earth, with its weight of lost human souls. How such a situation ever came about requires our deepest powers of understanding. That man is in reality a cosmic being also, spending only a part of his existence here on the Earth, needs to be included in the great range of ideas that belongs to Christianity today. Christ Himself, a divine Being who knows what it is to be human, has made the Earth the place not only of His dwelling but of His continuing history and evolution. He is a Being of the past, the present and the future, who brings the power of the future into our human life on Earth that we may likewise evolve. If religion is treated as a thing of the past, the most important part of the life of Christ is missed. It is related to the future and the further becoming of ourselves, as God's children, waking up to ourselves in the far country of the Earth. The elder brother in the parable of the prodigal son did not understand the adventure of Earth existence. But in the background to this picture there stands another Son, who looks for the prodigal one in the far country to show him his true home.

8

The third task of a priest in the Christian Community is pastoral care, which is frequently called counselling. In the past this task was concerned with sin, although this is no longer so today. Sins were once confessed to a priest in order to get rid of them. It was felt that the Church would take on the burden of sins given over in confession to the priest. In pronouncing the absolution, the priest was believed to be lifting the weight of sin from the wrongdoer and allowing him to go out into the world free of any responsibility. But what of the egohood and the sense of responsibility which should be preserved? The Church at that time could almost be described as a mother hen stretching out her wings to shelter helpless chickens. But the situation has changed.

The first step in a pastoral conversation should be to bring about understanding on both a higher and lower level. The one who asks for such a conversation need not feel guilty or sinful; he may be at a turning point in his destiny and wish to look ahead. It is not the priest but the one who comes who will decide the subject of the consultation, or where a problem begins or ends. The one who listens has undertaken not to speak of what he has heard. There must never be a confusion between gossip, or tea and sympathy, with pastoral care. It is a far greater problem for those who wish to practise counselling out of their kind hearts than that which is undertaken against a religious background. The counsellor takes upon himself the responsibility of looking at an action, or words said, which are still part of a real situation, and leading the other into his true responsibility and awareness of egohood. No Church today can take over that which belongs to the individual person but it can arouse in him the hope of understanding the problem and its consequences. The act of understanding does not relieve the responsibility. The question now is what can be done to meet it, what is the motive of the one to whom it belongs and what consequences can be foreseen. The priest may be far-sighted enough to suggest a solution. On the other hand the one who comes may be so relieved by baring his soul that he may be able to see the solution himself. He may resolve to do that which he could not have foreseen alone; it may even happen that both together foresee the next step forward and the one who has come goes forth with new courage.

The solution will be that which is so appropriate to the situation that it will bring courage and relief to all the people concerned. In other words, true forgiveness appears out of trouble. If we look at the first part of the Bible, many examples can be found of revenge and retribution; an old state of consciousness is revealed. In that pre-Christian time, revenge was considered courageous and forgiveness weak. 'Shall I be so base as to forgive my enemies,' cried one warrior in an old Greek story. In fact, the principle of an eye for an eye and a tooth for a tooth seems from that point of view to recommend no restraint; the wrongdoer should meet the exact consequences of his actions. With the New Testament, Christ brought into the world quite a new principle. Forgiveness is no longer base but a truly creative force in the progress of history. New situations can arise, changes of heart become effective, and the old logic is replaced by the new logic for the future. In the new conditions of existence, the ego of a human being can foresee, go into action and produce the new which can transform the old. His forgiveness requires courage, but it also gives courage and allows for new courageous solutions.

But how will this happen? It is well known that good intentions alone are not enough. Among the many new Christian ideas that Rudolf Steiner brought into the world is his conception of karma. The word 'karma' became well known before his time, through the ideas coming from the East. It once meant the just and logical consequences of a deed falling back upon the doer after a lengthy period of time. It is summed up in the old proverb that he who takes to the sword will perish by the sword. But new meaning can be added to the concept of karma, or destiny, by the change wrought by the presence of Christ. Karma begins to have within it the working of divine Grace; it creates opportunities for those who have wronged each other to bring about new situations, either from an act of forgiveness or from the experience of being forgiven. It makes necessary imaginative concepts that can transform old situations. Forgiveness is not a weakness—it is the strength to produce opportunities for transformation. The divine spiritual Beings who weave the patterns in human destiny need not overwhelm the ego; they call upon it to shape new patterns of opportunity. According to Rudolf Steiner, karma is transformed into the power to produce the new instruments of forgiveness. Through the coming of Christ, each person can redeem himself by fulfilling the opportunities that are given to him by his destiny. He will be enabled to achieve what is most difficult—to forgive himself.

The purpose of pastoral care is to find the means of working with the principle of forgiveness—willingness, understanding and the moral imagination to set the process in motion, which will make real the intention to forgive. The way in which the priest listens may make it possible for the one who comes to recognize for himself what he can do. The blessing in the words of the ritual with which the conversation is concluded are then said by him or her. That which a person imagines for himself and for which he takes responsibility is that which makes the most impression on him, rousing his courage. But many situations are not as simple as that. The capacity for moral imagination and for acting on it may, at any stage in the process, be insufficient. The priest who listens may have to contribute to the fulfilment of the process. Although offering advice is not the first aim of the pastor, it may be necessary to give more help. In every situation the first aim should be to see that the one who comes finds his own way to a decision. The technique is not to advise but to call up imaginative pictures in the person who comes. A further question can now be put: is this a task for a woman priest?

It might well be argued that a sympathetic woman is likely to be in a more favourable position. But she will experience the dangers of her own feminine tendencies. One particular difficulty in pastoral care is often encountered. Some of those with this task are inclined to present pictures of what they do themselves. They easily tend to believe that the problems that they have solved are the same as other people's and their good solution should be good for everyone. This is the danger produced by the kind of thinking recommended in the last century by the philosopher Kant. Even if his books are not widely read, there are many who favour his way of thinking. He recommended that a person should so act that when his action is good in his case it would be good and right for everyone who copied him. No doubt a policeman on traffic duty would recommend that everyone followed the example of the good driver, but traffic regulations must be maintained in common to prevent collisions. Quite justifiably, a policeman once complained to a driver that if her car had 12 horse power, then six of her horses were going one way and six another, which could only produce a catastrophe. There are conditions in modern life where rules and regulations are inevitable. But there are other decisions, which should depend on the moral imagination of the individual person.

There was once a pastor who had arranged, as he believed, an excellent working arrangement with his wife as to how they should share their common life. Both were hard-working people. He was once consulted by a lady from fashionable circles whose husband was in the diplomatic service. He had great charm but no feeling for fidelity. This pastor outlined the arrangements he made with his wife and suggested to the distressed lady that she should follow the pattern set up by himself, ignoring the fact that their circumstances were entirely different. This Kantian solution was quite inappropriate. In this case, a masculine pastor is being described whose method would be unlikely to be followed by a woman priest. More insight into the differences between people and greater skill in imagination is often found, but not always, in the female in contrast to the male. On the other hand, the woman counsellor may be tempted to be too personally involved with those whom she counsels. Objectivity is important, although it may have to be sought in different ways. One lady said to me that although she wished to give up her sessions in counselling she couldn't do so because the counsellor would miss her too much!

In such matters, women are much more likely to be ready and patient in the fulfilling of the tasks of pastoral care. This is a generalization, and liable to exceptions of course. However, it would not be possible on any reasonable grounds to object to women becoming priests in this area. Priests have a threefold task and, in spite of the old traditions, the time has come when the work of the priest depends upon the active ego within the individual person. Quotations from past circumstances are therefore inappropriate. There are, in current discussions on the subject of women priests, 'a lot of non-verifiable opinions about verbal meanings' (*Guardian*, 11 September 1991).

The task of the priest requires endurance. The ability to carry it out develops with experience and continual efforts. Hard as it may be to imagine, devotion to the same task for a lifetime is of profound importance. There are many and varied aspects to all that belongs to this calling. There is no risk of repetition for anyone who deals with such a variety of possibilities, for a priest can take up different ways of working: in literature, art, music, psychology or spiritual science. He can look for different experiences of people, of places, of languages, or he can be satisfied with specializing in the place where he is, because in that situation he can satisfy better the needs of the whole movement. A correct balance between his own inclinations, the needs of his work and the well-being of the whole Church needs to be cultivated if his ministry is to be satisfactory. Devotion and unselfishness are needed if his mission is to be benevolent. Continual thought and care are necessary, through the years, for the work he undertakes. In modern circumstances this presents a difficulty for those who look for continual change. A balance is struck where the sense of vocation and the deeper experience of the value of the work are available.

Religion goes in and out of fashion in the course of history. But those who can recognize the value in the modern human being of that which has been described as 'Homo religiosus' will be aware that, underneath the phases of fashion, the eternal soul in human beings persists and will make itself felt.

Notes

1. Born the son of a humble Austrian station-master, Rudolf Steiner (1861–1925) has achieved world fame as the father of Anthroposophy and a pioneer of genius in many different fields. He brought challenging new insights into such varied disciplines as medicine, science, education (Waldorf schools), special education, philosophy, religion, architecture, drama, agriculture (Bio-Dynamic method), economics, the new art of eurythmy, and many others. He founded the General Anthroposophical Society in 1923 and there are now many branches throughout the world which testify to the growing reputation of this remarkable man.
2. Dr Friedrich Rittelmeyer, born in 1872, became a leading clergyman of the German Lutheran Church. A minister at one of the best-known Berlin churches and a popular preacher, he was so well known he could fill the biggest churches and lecture halls. He met Steiner in 1911 at a theosophical conference in Munich. In the autumn of 1921 he joined a circle of Christian Community aspirants. In 1922, he resigned from the Lutheran Church and became the first Head of the Christian Community, an international movement for religious renewal. He died in 1938.

    Rittelmeyer was the author of several books, including the following (in English translation): *Rudolf Steiner Enters My Life* (The Christian Community Press, London, 1929); *Meditation— Letters on the Guidance of the Inner Life* (The Christian Community Press, London, 1948); *Reincarnation* (first published by The Christian Community Press, 1933, reprinted by Floris Books, Edinburgh, 1988).
3. Rudolf Steiner made several references to Mary, the Madonna, in his lectures. For example: lectures of 4–5 August 1908 in *Universe, Earth and Man*; 29 April 1909, in *Isis and Sophia*; 29 July 1923, in *Colour*; 6 October 1923, in *The Four Seasons and the Archangels* and 14 December 1923, in *Mystery Knowledge and Mystery Centres*. See also lectures of 3–4 July 1909 in *The Gospel of St John and its Relation to the Other Three Gospels*.

4. For the Egyptian 'Cinderella', see *Tales of Ancient Egypt*, an authoritative collection of the myths, folk tales and legends of ancient Egypt, selected and retold by Roger Lancelyn Green (Puffin Books).
5. On Celtic Christianity, see *The Flaming Door*, by Eleanor C. Merry (New Knowledge Books, London, 1967). *Historia Ecclesiastica Gentis Anglorum* (Ecclesiastical History of the English People) is Bede's most celebrated work; *The Venerable Bede and His Ecclesiastical History*, by Lady Gregory, covers the main details in Chapter 3.
6. On Abélard, Helen Waddell, *The Wandering Scholars* (Constable, 1933), and, for translations of some of his verse, *Mediaeval Latin Lyrics* (Constable, 1929). Also by Helen Waddell is the novel *Abélard and Héloïse*.
7. There are many references in Steiner's lectures to the Ego Consciousness. The following is a selection from those that relate to its beginning and development: 13 April 1909, in *The Spiritual Hierarchies*; 14 June 1910, in *The Mission of Folk-Souls*; 23 April 1912, in *Cosmic and Earthly Man*; 20 November 1912, in *Between Death and Rebirth*; 7 August 1908, in *Universe, Earth and Man*; 26 August 1911, in *Wonders of the World*. See also *Karmic Relationships*, Vol. I, p. 98; *From Symptom to Reality*, p. 77; *Manifestations of Karma*, p. 143; *Occult Physiology*, p. 91; *The World as Product of Balance*, p. 36; and *The New Spirituality and the Christ Experience of the Twentieth Century*.
8. There are a number of books by, and about, Stevie Smith. Her last one was *Me Again* (Virago Press).
9. Jacob's ladder—see Genesis 28:12.
10. The hymn 'O Brother Man . . .' is No. 307 in *Songs of Praise*. The words are by J.G. Whittier (1807-92) and the music by Parry.
11. On St Brendan and voyages to America, see Steiner's lectures of 15-16 November 1917, in *Geographic Medicine* (Mercury Press, Spring Valley, New York).
12. On the subject of reincarnation and Christianity, one of the best books available is *Reincarnation*, by Friedrich Rittelmeyer (see Note 2).